Packets of Sunlight
For
American Patriots

Compiled by Marnie L. Pehrson

If you enjoy this book, you'll also enjoy
Packets of Sunlight for Parents
http://www.SheLovesGod.com/parents

Published by C.E.S. Business Consultants
Tel: 706-866-2295 * webmaster@SheLovesGod.com
http://www.SheLovesGod.com/packets

Artwork from Microsoft Clipart Gallery
and *Quest of the Hemisphere* by
Donzella C. Boyle, Western Islands, 1970

ISBN 0-9676162-3-9

Preface

Richard G. Scott said that the Lord, "will place in your path *packets of spiritual sunlight to brighten your way*. They often come after the trial has been the greatest, as evidence of the compassion and love of an all-knowing Father. They point the way to greater happiness, more understanding, and strengthen your determination to accept and be obedient to His will." (Richard G. Scott "Trust in the Lord" November 1994 Ensign, p.17)

In the troubled times in which we live, we would do well to return to the values and principles upon which our country was founded. The freedoms vouchsafed within the U.S. Constitution and the God who inspired our Forefathers are what has carried us through these hundreds of years, and what we must return to and rely upon if we wish our grandchildren and great-grandchildren to live in freedom as well.

This collection of patriotic packets of sunlight has been a long time in coming and is something I wanted to do in honor of my father, Jack Morton, who is the greatest friend to freedom I know. He taught me to love my country and to understand the freedoms protected in the U.S. Constitution. Hopefully this collection will inspire others to share that love and understanding as well.

I hope you enjoy!

Marnie L. Pehrson

Table of Contents

I Pledge Allegiance

Patriotism Defined

"What do we mean by patriotism in the context of our times?... A patriotism that puts country ahead of self; a patriotism which is not short, frenzied outbursts of emotion, but the tranquil and steady dedication of a lifetime." (Adlai Stevenson, speech given in New York City, 27 August 1952, quoted in John Bartlett, *Familiar Quotations*, Boston: Little, Brown and Co., p. 1955, p. 986)

𝔇𝔢𝔡𝔦𝔠𝔞𝔱𝔦𝔬𝔫 𝔬𝔣 𝔞 𝔩𝔦𝔣𝔢𝔱𝔦𝔪𝔢

All That I Have and All That I Am

"Sink or swim, live or die, survive or perish, I give my hand and my heart to this
vote. It is true, indeed, that in the beginning
we aimed not at independence. But there's
a divinity which shapes our ends... Why,
then, should we defer the Declaration?

"You and I, indeed, may rue it. We may
not live to the time when this Declaration
shall be made good... but whatever may be
our fate, be assured, ... that this Declaration
will stand. It may cost treasure, and it may
cost blood: but it will stand, and it will
richly compensate for both...

"My judgement approves this measure,
and my whole heart is in it. All that I have,
and all that I am, and all that I hope, in this
life, I am now ready here to stake upon it;
and I leave off as I began, that live or die,
survive or perish, I am for the Declaration.
It is my living sentiment, and by the blessing of God it shall be my dying sentiment,
independence, now, and independence
forever." (Daniel Webster, *The Works of
Daniel Webster*, 4th ed., 1851, 1:133-36.)

"These are the times that try men's souls. The summer soldier and the sunshine patriot will in this crisis, shrink from the service of his country; but he that stands it now, deserves the love and thanks of man and woman. Tyranny, like hell, is not easily conquered; yet we have this consolation with us, that the harder the conflict, the more glorious the triumph. What we obtain too cheap, we esteem too lightly; 'tis dearness only that gives everything its value. Heaven knows how to put a proper price upon its goods; and it would be strange indeed, if so celestial an article as freedom should not be highly rated." (Thomas Paine, *The American Crisis*, no. 1, 1776)

freedom: celestial article

"God provided that in this land of liberty, our political allegiance shall run not to individuals, that is, to government officials, no matter how great or how small they may be. Under His plan our allegiance and the only allegiance we owe as citizens or denizens of the United States, runs to our inspired Constitution which God himself set up. So runs the oath of office of those who participate in government. A certain loyalty we do owe to the office which a man holds, but even here we owe just by reason of our citizenship, no loyalty to the man himself. In other countries it is to the individual that allegiance runs. This principle of allegiance to the Constitution is basic to our freedom. It is one of the great principles that distinguishes this land of liberty from other countries." (J. Reuben Clark, Jr., *Stand Fast by Our Constitution*, Deseret Book, 1962, p. 189)

allegiance to Constitution

Theodore Roosevelt

"Patriotism means to stand by the country. It does not mean to stand by the President or any other public official save exactly to the degree in which he himself stands by the country...

"Every man who parrots the cry of 'stand by the President' without adding the proviso 'so far as he serves the Republic' takes an attitude as essentially unmanly as that of any Stuart royalist who championed the doctrine that the King could do no wrong. No self-respecting and intelligent free man could take such an attitude." (Theodore Roosevelt, *Works*, vol. 21, pp. 316, 321).

To the Flag

When Freedom, from her mountain height,
      Unfurled her standard to the air,
She tore the azure robe of night,
      And set the stars of glory there;
She mingled with its gorgeous dyes
The milky baldric of the skies,
And striped its pure, celestial white
With streakings of the morning light;
Then from his mansion in the sun,
She called her eagle-bearer down,
And gave into his mighty hand
The symbol of her chosen land.

(Joseph Rodman Drake, in *The World's Best
Loved Poems*, James G. Lawson, ed., pp. 287-
288.)

symbol of her chosen land

A Symbol of Freedom

"A Symbol is an object which represents something, which, though equally real, is not tangible. The flag is a symbol. To destroy that symbol is to reject what it represents.

"The burning of the flag is an act which in itself becomes symbolic. It symbolizes the rejection of the Pledge of Allegiance. The Bill of Rights guarantees freedom of speech. Speech is made up of spoken or printed words. Words are words are words. Acts are acts are acts.

"The willful destruction of the flag which belongs to all of us is the act of an extremist. A court decision legalizing the destruction of it to protect the rights of one protestor is equally extreme." (Boyd K. Packer, *The Spirit of America*, p. 51-52, Bookcraft, 1998)

long may she wave...

The Star Spangled Banner
The Defense of Fort McHenry
by Francis Scott Key, 20 September 1814

Oh, say can you see, by the dawn's early light,
What so proudly we hailed at the twilight's last
*   gleaming?*
Whose broad stripes and bright stars, through the
*   perilous fight,*
O'er the ramparts we watched, were so gallantly
*   streaming?*
And the rockets' red glare, the bombs bursting in
*   air,*
Gave proof through the night that our flag was
*   still there.*
O say, does that star-spangled banner yet wave
O'er the land of the free and the home of the brave?

On the shore, dimly seen through the mists of the
*   deep,*
Where the foe's haughty host in dread silence re-
*   poses,*
What is that which the breeze, o'er the towering
*   steep,*
As it fitfully blows, now conceals, now discloses?
Now it catches the gleam of the morning's first
*   beam,*
In full glory reflected now shines on the stream:
'Tis the star-spangled banner! O long may it wave
O'er the land of the free and the home of the brave.

And where is that band who so vauntingly swore
That the havoc of war and the battle's confusion
A home and a country should leave us no more?
Their blood has wiped out their foul footstep's pol-
*   lution.*
No refuge could save the hireling and slave
From the terror of flight, or the gloom of the grave:
And the star-spangled banner in triumph doth
*   wave*
O'er the land of the free and the home of the brave.

Oh! thus be it ever, when freemen shall stand
Between their loved homes and the war's desola-
*   tion!*
Blest with victory and peace, may the heaven-res-
*   cued land*
Praise the Power that hath made and preserved us
a nation.
Then conquer we must, for our cause it is just,
And this be our motto: "In God is our trust."
And the star-spangled banner forever shall wave
O'er the land of the free and the home of the brave!

*'Tis fine to see the Old World, and travel up and
    down.*
Among the famous palaces and cities of renown,
*To admire the crumbly castles and the statues of
    the kings, --*
*But now I think I've had enough of antiquated
    things.*

*So it's home again, and home again, America for
    me!*
*My heart is turning home again, and there I long
    to be*
*In the land of youth and freedom beyond the
    ocean bars,*
*Where the air is full of sunlight and the flag is
    full of stars.*

- Henry Van Dyke

The History of the Flag
of the United States
by William J. Canby of Philadelphia

"Sitting sewing in her shop one day with her girls around her, several gentlemen entered. Betsy recognized one of these as the uncle of her deceased husband, Col. GEORGE ROSS, a delegate from Pennsylvania to Congress. She also knew the handsome form and features of the dignified, yet graceful and polite Commander in Chief, who, while he was yet COLONEL WASHINGTON had visited her shop both professionally and socially many times, (a friendship caused by her connection with the Ross family). They announced themselves as a committee of congress, and stated that they had been appointed to prepare a flag, and asked her if she thought she could make one, to which she replied, with her usual modesty and self reliance, that 'she did not know but she could try; she had never made one but if the pattern were shown to her she had no doubt of her

ability to do it.' The committee were shown into her back parlor, the room back of the shop, and Col. Ross produced a drawing, roughly made, of the proposed flag. It was defective to the clever eye of Mrs. Ross and unsymmetrical, and she offered suggestions which Washington and the committee readily approved.

What all these suggestions were we cannot definitely determine, but they were of sufficient importance to involve an alteration and redrawing of the design, which was then and there done by General George Washington, in pencil, in her back parlor. One of the alterations had reference to the shape of the stars. In the drawing they were made with six points. Mrs. Ross at once said that this was wrong; the stars should be five pointed; they were aware of that, but thought there would be some difficulty in making a five pointed star. 'Nothing easier' was her prompt reply and folding a piece of paper in the proper manner, with one clip of her ready scissors she quickly displayed to their astonished vision the five pointed star; which accordingly took its place in the national standard. General Washington was the active one in making the design, the others having little or nothing to do with it. When it was completed, it was given to William Barrett, painter, to paint.

He had no part in the design, he only did the painting. (He was a first rate artist. He lived in a large three story brick house on the East side of an alley which ran back to the Pennsylvania Academy for young ladies, which was kept by James A Neal; said to be the best institution of the kind at that time in Philadelphia. The house is yet standing.)

The committee suggested Mrs. Ross to call at a certain hour at the counting house of one of their number, a shipping merchant, on the wharf. Mrs. Ross was punctual to the appointment. The gentleman drew out of a chest an old ship's color, which he loaned her to show her how the sewing was done, and also the drawing painted by Barrett. Other designs had been prepared by the committee and one or two of them were placed in the hands of other seamstresses to be made. Betsy Ross went diligently to work upon her flag, carefully examining the peculiar stitch in the old ship's color, which had been given her as a specimen, and recognizing, with the eye of a good mechanic its important characteristics, strength and elasticity.

The flag was soon finished, and Betsy returned it, the first 'Star Spangled Banner' that ever floated upon the breeze, to her employer. It was run up to the peak of one of his ships lying at the wharf, and received the unanimous approval of the committee and of a little group of bystanders looking on, and the same day was carried into the State House and laid before Congress, with a report from the committee.

The next day Col. Ross called upon Betsy, and informed her that her work had been approved and her flag adopted; and he now requested her to turn her whole attention to the manufacture of flags, and gave her an unlimited order for as many as she could make; desiring her to go out forthwith and buy all the 'bunting and tack' in the city, and make flags as fast as possible. Here was astounding mews [sic] to Betsy! Her largest ideas of business heretofore had been confined to the furnishing of one or two houses at a time with beds, curtains and carpets; and she had only recently been depressed with the prospect of losing much of this limited business by reason of the high prices of materials, and the consequent retrenchment by citizens in luxuries that could be dispensed with. She sat ruminating upon her sudden good fortune some minutes before it occurred to her that she had not the means to make the extensive purchases required by the order; and, therefore, she would be utterly help-less to fill it; for these were the days of cash transactions, and such a thing as a poor person getting credit for a large amount of goods was altogether unheard of. Here was a dilemma. What was she to do? Like many others, she began already to doubt her good fortune and to dash her rising hopes with the reflections, 'this is too good luck for me, it cannot be.' Rising superior to this, however, she said to herself, 'We are not creatures of luck: have I not found that the Good One has never deserted me, and He will not now. I will buy all the bunting I can, and make it into these flags, and will explain to Mr. Ross why I cannot get any-more. He will, no doubt, give orders to others, and so I shall lose a large part of this business: but I must be satisfied with a moderate share of it, and grateful too.'

So she went to work. Scarcely had she

finished her cogitations when Col. Ross reentered the shop. 'It was very thoughtless of me' he remarked, 'when I was just here now, that I did not offer to supply you with the means for making these purchases; it might inconvenience you' he said delicately, 'to pay out so much cash at once, here is something to begin with' (giving her a one hundred pound note) 'and you must draw on me at sight for what ever you require.'

Mrs. Ross was now effectively set up in the business of flag and color making for the government; through all her after life, which was a long, useful and eventful one, she 'never knew what it was,' to use her own expression, 'to want employment,' this business (flag-making for the government) remaining with her and in her family for many years. She was afterwards twice married; once to Joseph Ashbourne, a shipmaster in the merchant services, by whom she had one daughter, named Eliza, and after his death to John Claypoole."

(A Paper read before the Historical Society of Pennsylvania (in 1870. More information found at http://www.ushistory.org/betsy/more/canby.htm)

Of the United States of America

"America united, with a handful of troops, or without a single soldier, exhibits a more forbidding posture to foreign ambition than America disunited, with a hundred thousand veterans ready for combat... A dangerous establishment can never be necessary or plausible, so long as they continue a united people. But let it never for a moment be forgotten that they are indebted for this advantage to the Union alone. The moment of its dissolution will be the date of the new order of things... It will present liberty everywhere crushed between standing armies and perpetual taxes...

"This picture of the consequences of disunion cannot be too highly colored, or too often exhibited. Every man who loves peace, every man who loves his country, every man who loves liberty ought to cherish in his heart a due attachment to the Union of America and be able to set a due value on the means of preserving it." (James Madison, as quoted in W. Cleon Skousen's *The Making of America*, p. 238)

𝔄merica united

"The powers not delegated to the United
States by the Constitution, nor prohibited
by it to the States, are reserved to the States
respectively, or to the people."

- U.S. Constitution
10th Amendment

reserved to the States
or the people

Return to the Fine Highway

"The complexity of social organization does not change. Our technologically sophisticated industrial society is more complex than the agrarian society of America in the eighteenth century. In this regard, that was "a simpler world." But the complexities of politics (*politics* here meaning the *science of governing*) do not change much. The basic political problems confronting the Framers of our Constitution were as complex as our political problems today -- perhaps more so, because they were striking off into the dangerous unknown, whereas all we need do is return to the fine highway we were once on."
(Lawrence Patton McDonald, *We Hold These Truths, p. 13, '76 Press, 1976)*

as complex then as now

The Federal Government Shall Not...

"The words, *the federal government shall not*, run through our Bill of Rights like a refrain. This was the spirit of liberty, the keystone of our greatness. But the Bill of Rights operates only against federal power. It does not affect state power. It prohibits no action by state governments, orders none, and provides the people no protection against usurpation by the various states...

"Under the principles of English common law which were grafted into the first eight amendments of the American Bill of Rights, every person has inviolable rights to certain things (freedom of speech, assembly, religion). If he illegally harms others in the exercise of any of these rights, he is subject to punishment, after fair and impartial trial, by the government to which he is answerable for his private activities.

"That is why the Founding Fathers directed the Bill of Rights *exclusively* at the federal government: people were to be answerable for their private activities only to the state authority, except with regard to powers which the Constitution clearly gives to the federal government."
(Lawrence Patton McDonald, *We Hold These Truths, p. 39,41-42, '76 Press, 1976)*

George Washington

A Miracle

"It appears to me, then, little short of a miracle, that the delegates from so many different states (which states you know are also different from each other in their manners, circumstances and prejudices) should unite in forming a system of national Government, so little liable to well-founded objections." (Letter from Washington to Lafayette, 7 Feb. 1788, quoted in Chaterine Drinker Bowen, *Miracle at Philadelphia*, Boston: Little, Brown, and Co., 1966, p. xvii)

little short of a miracle

"The success of the [Constitutional] convention was attributable in large part to the
remarkable intelligence, wisdom, and
unselfishness of the delegates" (Dallin H.
Oaks, *The Spirit of America*, p. 15, Bookcraft,
1998)

"There never was an assembly of men,
charged with a great and arduous trust,
who were more pure in their motives, or
more exclusively or anxiously devoted to
the object committed to them." (James
Madison, quoted in William O. Nelson, *The
Charter of Liberty*, Salt Lake City: Deseret
Book Co., 1987, p. 44)

pure in motives

Benjamin Franklin
1706-1790

"When you assemble a number of men to have the advantage over their joint wisdom, you inevitably assemble with those men all their prejudices, their passions, their errors of opinion, their local interests, and their selfish views. From such an assembly can a perfect production be expected? It therefore astonishes me, Sir, to find this system approaching so near to perfection as it does... The opinions I have had of its errors, I sacrifice to the public good." (Benjamin Franklin, *Notes of Debates in the Federal Convention of 1787 Reported by James Madison*, p. 653, quoted in Nelson, *The Charter of Liberty*, p. 57)

so near to perfection

"We owe every other sacrifice to ourselves, to our federal brethren, and to the world at large to pursue with temper and persever-ance the great experiment which shall prove that man is capable of living in a society governing itself by laws self-im-posed, and securing to its members the enjoyment of life, liberty, property and peace; and further, to show that even when the government of its choice shall manifest a tendency to degeneracy, we are not at once to despair, but that the will and the watchfulness of its sounder parts will reform its aberrations, recall it to original and legitimate principles, and restrain it within the rightful limits of self-govern-ment." (Thomas Jefferson, as quoted in W. Cleon Skousen's, *The Making of America*, pp.238-239)

remain united

"This government never of itself furthered any enterprise, but by the alacrity with which it got out of its way. *It* does not keep the country free. *It* does not settle the West. *It* does not educate. The character inherent in the American people has done all that has been accomplished; and it would have done somewhat more, if the government had not sometimes got in its way. For government is an expedient by which men would fain succeed in letting one another alone; and, as has been said, when it is most expedient, the governed are most let alone by it." (Henry D. Thoreau, *Civil Disobedience*, 1849)

American character

And to the Republic for which it stands

James Madison
1751-1836

"Hence it is that democracies have ever been spectacles of turbulence and contention; have ever been found incompatible with personal security or the rights of property; and in general have been as short in their lives as they have been violent in their deaths... A republic, by which I mean a government in which a scheme of representation takes place, opens a different prospect and promises the cure for which we are seeking." (James Madison, Federalist Papers, the McClean Edition, Federalist Paper #10, page 81, 1788)

a different prospect

"This is a new event in the history of mankind. Heretofore most governments have been formed by tyrants, and imposed on mankind by force. Never before did a people, in time of peace and tranquility, meet together by their representatives, and, with calm deliberation, frame for themselves a system of government." (Samuel Huntington, as quoted in W. Cleon Skousen's *The Making of America*, p. 194)

never done before

"Under the American Constitution a new structure of government was established on a much higher plane than either the parliamentary system or the confederation of states. It was a people's *constitutional republic*, where a certain amount of power was delegated to the states and a certain amount was delegated to the national government. There was a small dimension of power which they shared jointly. All other power was retained by the people. It is the delegation by the people of certain powers to the states and certain powers to the national government which we call 'dual federalism.'" (W. Cleon Skousen, *The Making of America*, p. 199, The National Center for Constitutional Studies, 1985)

constitutional republic

Republic with a Spiritual Foundation

"Ours is a representative republic with a Constitution in which is recognized the natural law and the natural rights of man. It is a republic with a spiritual foundation characterized by freedom -- freedom for the individual and for his society." (Ezra Taft Benson, *An Enemy Hath Done This*, page 97.)

a representative republic

Separation of Powers

"In dividing the federal government into three branches, the Framers of the Constitution not only created a means of balancing state power against federal power, but also a way to divide and balance federal power against itself. They knew the intrinsic nature of government: power is its essential ingredient, and love of power the primary motivation of governing officials. They were giving the federal government great power, and attempted to chain it down by telling it what it could and could not do. But what if it disobeyed?

The Constitution makes the three branches separate, but not independent. It provides overlapping responsibilities for all branches, and gives special prerogatives to each. This makes them rivals, each jealous of its own power. Each branch has the means to inhibit, if not prevent, the actions of the others. This rivalry was deliberately created, and it was intended to act as a restraint to keep any of the three branches from disobeying the Constitution."
(Lawrence Patton McDonald, *We Hold These Truths, p. 30-31,* '76 Press, 1976)

"All legislative Powers herein granted shall be vested in a Congress of the United States, which shall consist of a Senate and House of Representatives."

> U.S. Constitution
> Article 1, Section 1

"If *all* legislative (lawmaking) powers are vested in Congress, then one might ask what portion is vested in the Executive (the Presidency, Cabinet and Agencies)? None! If *all* lawmaking powers are vested in the Congress then how much is vested in the Judiciary (Supreme Court)? None!"

> - Dr. Jack Morton

Vested in Congress

"We hold these Truths to be self-evident, that all Men are created equal, that they are endowed by their Creator with certain unalienable Rights, that among these are Life, Liberty, and the Pursuit of Happiness. That to secure these Rights, Governments are instituted among Men, deriving their just Powers from the Consent of the Governed."

- Declaration of Independence

We hold these truths...

"The way to have good and safe government, is not to trust it all to one, but to
divide it among the many, distributing to
every one exactly the functions he is com-
petent to. Let the national government be
entrusted with the defense of the nation,
and its foreign and federal relations; the
State governments with the civil rights, law,
police, and administration of what concerns
the State generally; the counties with the
local concerns of the counties, and each
ward direct the interests within itself. It is
by dividing and subdividing these repub-
lics from the great national one down
through all its subordinations, until it ends
in the administration of every man's farm
by himself; by placing under every one
what his own eye may superintend, that all
will be done for the best. What has destroyed liberty and the rights of man in
every government which has ever existed
under the sun? The generalizing and con-
centrating all cares and powers into one
body." (Thomas Jefferson, letter to Joseph
C. Cabell, February 2, 1816)

divide & subdivide

Limited Government

"[The general welfare] clause had caused the first and greatest controversy at the Constitutional Convention. James Madison successfully led the opposition to proposals which would have put Congress in the role of promoting the general welfare as Congress saw fit. Madison said:

'If Congress can employ money indefinitely to the general welfare, and are the sole and supreme judges of the general welfare, they may take the care of religion into their own hands; they may appoint teachers in every State, county and parish and pay them out of their public treasury; they may take into their own hands the education of children, establishing in like manner schools throughout the Union; they may assume the provision of the poor... Were the power of Congress to be established in the latitude contended for, it would subvert the very foundations, and transmute the very nature of the limited Government established by the people of America.'" (Lawrence Patton McDonald, *We Hold These Truths, pp. 45-46,* '76 Press, 1976)

the foundations

"When a portion of wealth is transferred from the person who owns it -- without his consent and without compensation, and whether by force or by fraud -- to anyone who does not own it, then I say that property is violated; that an act of plunder is committed...

"How is this legal plunder to be identified? Quite simply. See if the law takes from some persons what belongs to them, and gives it to other persons to whom it does not belong. See if the law benefits one citizen at the expense of another by doing what the citizen himself cannot do without committing a crime..." (Fredrick Bastiat, *The Law*, p. 21, 26)

beware of legal plunder

"Assume for example, that we were farmers, and that we received a letter from the government telling us that we were going to get a thousand dollars this year for ploughed up acreage. But rather than the normal method of collection, we were to take this letter and collect $69.71 from Bill Brown, at such and such an address, and $82.47 from Henry Jones, $59.80 from a Bill Smith and so on down the line; that these men would make up our farm subsidy.

"Neither you nor I, nor would 99 percent of the farmers walk up and ring a man's doorbell, hold out a hand and say, 'Give me what you've earned even though I have not.' We simply wouldn't do it because we would be facing directly the violation of a moral law, 'Thou shalt not steal.' In short, we would be held accountable for our actions." (James R. Evans, *The Glorious Quest*, 1848)

what's immoral for one, is immoral for many

"With all of its weaknesses, our free enterprise system has accomplished in terms of
human welfare that which no other economic or social system has ever ap-
proached. Our freedom of individual
opportunity permits us to draw upon our
natural resources and upon the total brain
and brawn power of the nation in a most
effective manner. This freedom of individual choice inspires competition. Competition inspires shrewd and efficient man-
agement, which is conducive to the production of the best product possible at the
lowest price." (Ezra Taft Benson, *God,
Family, Country*, p. 310, Deseret Book Com-
pany, 1974)

free enterprise system

"Self-government involves self-control, self-discipline, an acceptance of and the most unremitting obedience to correct principles... No other form of government requires so high a degree of individual morality." (Albert E. Bowen, *Improvement Era*, vol. 41 [1938], p. 266)

self-government

One Nation,
Under God

"The man must be bad indeed who can look upon the events of the American Revolution without feeling the warmest gratitude toward the great Author of the Universe whose divine interposition was so frequently manifested in our behalf. And it is my earnest prayer that we may so conduct ourselves as to merit a continuance of those blessings with which we have hitherto been favored."

- George Washington

divine interposition

"If my people, which are called by my name, shall humble themselves, and pray, and seek my face, and turn from their wicked ways; then will I hear from heaven, and will forgive their sin, and will heal their land."

- 2 Chronicles 7:14

heal their land

If A Sparrow Cannot Fall,
A Nation Cannot Rise

"I have lived sir, a long time, and the longer I live, the more convincing proofs I see of this truth, that God governs in the affairs of men. And, if a sparrow cannot fall to the ground without his notice is it probable that an empire can rise without his aid? We have been assured, sir, in the sacred writings, that 'except the Lord build the house, they labor in vain that build it.;

"I firmly believe this; and I also believe, that, without his concurring aid, we shall succeed in this political building no better than the builders of Babel;...

"I therefore beg leave to move, that henceforth prayers, imploring the assistance of heaven, and its blessings on our deliberations, be held in this assembly every morning before we proceed to business: and that one or more of the clergy of this city be requested to officiate in that service." (Benjamin Franklin as quoted by Jared Sparks, *The Works of Benjamin Franklin,* 1837, pp. 155-56)

Separation of Church & State

"I support the doctrine of separation of church and state as traditionally interpreted to prohibit the establishment of an official national religion. But this does not mean that we should divorce government from any formal recognition of God. To do so strikes a potentially fatal blow at the concept of the divine origin of our rights, and unlocks the door for an easy entry of future tyranny. If Americans should ever come to believe that their rights and freedoms are instituted among men by politicians and bureaucrats, they will no longer carry the proud inheritance of their forefathers, but will grovel before their masters seeking favors and dispensations -- a throwback to the feudal system of the Dark Ages." (Ezra Taft Benson, "Freedom Is Our Heritage," 10 Nov. 1970)

stiking a fatal blow

Charles Cotesworth Pinckney
1746-1825

"When the great work was done and published, I was...struck with amazement.
Nothing less than that superintending hand
of Providence, that so miraculously carried
us through the war... could have brought it
about so complete, upon the whole."
(Charles Pinckney speaking of the U.S.
Constitution, P.L. Ford, ed., *Essays on the
Constitution*, 1892, p. 412)

struck with amazement

George Washington

"Of all the dispositions and habits which lead to political prosperity, religion and morality are indispensable supports... Reason and experience both forbid us to expect that national morality can prevail in exclusion of religious principles."

- George Washington
  Farewell address

indispensable supports

John Jay, the first Chief Justice of the Supreme Court and one of the three men most responsible for the U.S. Constitution stated, "Providence has given to our people the choice of their rulers, and it is the duty - as well as the privilege and interest - of our Christian nation to select and prefer Christians for their rulers."

Christian nation

"Why is it that next to the birthday of the Savior of the world, your most venerated festival returns on this day? Is it not that in the chain of human events, the birthday of the nation is indissolubly linked with the birthday of the Savior? That it forms a leading event in the progress of the gospel dispensation? Is it not that the Declaration of Independence first organized the social compact on the foundation of the Redeemer's mission upon the earth? That it laid the cornerstone of human government upon the first precepts of Christianity?"

- John Quincy Adams
  July 4, 1837 Address

gospel dispensation

Abraham Lincoln
President from 1861-1865

"God rules this world. It is the duty of
nations as well as men to owe their depen-
dence upon the overruling power of God,
to confess their sins and transgressions in
humble sorrow... and to recognize the
sublime truths that those nations only are
blessed whose God is the Lord."

- Abraham Lincoln

𝔱𝔥𝔬𝔰𝔢 𝔫𝔞𝔱𝔦𝔬𝔫𝔰 𝔬𝔫𝔩𝔶

George Mason
1725-1792

"As nations cannot be rewarded or punished in the next world, so they must be in this. By an inevitable chain of causes and effects, Providence punishes national sins by national calamities."

- George Mason
  Father of the Bill of Rights

chain of causes & effects

"'Blessed is the nation whose God is the Lord."

> *- Psalms 33:12*

"'Righteousness exalteth a nation; but sin is a reproach to any people."

> *- Proverbs 14:34*

"But the nation and kingdom that will not serve [God] shall perish; yea, those nations shall be utterly destroyed."

> *- Isaiah 60:12*

blessed is the nation

"The success, which has hitherto attended
our united efforts, we owe to the gracious
interposition of heaven, and to that interposition let us gratefully ascribe the praise of
victory, and the blessings of peace."
(George Washington, To the Executives of
New Hampshire, November 3, 1789)

Ay, call it holy ground,
        The soil where they first trod,
They have left unstained what they found--
        Freedom to worship God.

        - Felicia Dorothea Hemans

interposition of heaven

"Just think for a moment of George Washington, of Franklin, of Madison, of the Adamses, of Patrick Henry, Thomas Jefferson and their associates who signed the Declaration of Independence or participated in the Constitutional Convention. Where in all the world today can even one or two such men be found, let alone the great aggregation who participated in the birth of America?

"Can anyone deny that they were raised up unto this very purpose, that working together they brought forth on this continent an independent nation, at the risk of their lives, their fortunes, and their sacred honor?

"It is my conviction that while we have had a few great leaders since then, there has not been before or since so large a group of talented, able and dedicated men as those whom we call the founding fathers of our nation.

"For as long as they lived, they acknowledged the hand of the Almighty in the affairs of this republic." (Gordon B. Hinckley, *The Spirit of America*, p. 153, Bookcraft, 1998)

raised up by God

James Madison
1751-1836

"It is impossible for the man of pious reflection not to perceive in it [the Constitution] a finger of that Almighty hand which has been so frequently and signally extended to our relief in the critical stages of the revolution." (James Madison, *The Federalist*, No. 37)

finger of Almighty hand

Indivisible

"I now make it my earnest prayer, that God would incline the hearts of the citizens to cultivate a spirit of subordination and obedience to government, to entertain a brotherly affection and love for one another,...and finally, that he would most graciously be pleased to dispose us all, to do justice, to love mercy, and to demean ourselves with that charity, humility and pacific temper of mind, which were the characteristics of the Divine Author of our blessed religion, and without an humble imitation of whose example in these things, we can never hope to be a happy nation."

- George Washington

do justice, love mercy

The Source of America's Greatness

In the nineteenth century a young French-man, Alexis de Tocqueville, came to the United States to observe this nation. After-wards he wrote:

"I sought for the greatness and genius of America in her commodious harbors and her ample rivers, and it was not there; in her fertile fields and boundless prairies, and it was not there; in her rich mines and her vast world commerce, and it was not there. Not until I went to the churches of America and heard her pulpits aflame with righteousness did I understand the secret of her genius and power. America is great because she is good, and if America ever ceases to be good, America will cease to be great." (Quoted in *The Spirit of America*, p32, Bookcraft 1998)

secret of her genius

"We have staked the whole future of American civilization not upon the power of government -- far from it. We have staked the future of all of our political institutions upon the capacity of each and all of us to govern ourselves according to the Ten Commandments of God." (James Madison, Russ Walton, *Biblical Principles of Importance to Godly Christians* [New Hampshire: Plymouth Foundation, 1984], p. 361)

to govern ourselves

"And it shall come to pass, if thou shalt hearken diligently unto the voice of the LORD thy God, to observe and to do all his commandments which I command thee this day, that the LORD thy God will set thee on high above all nations of the earth:

And all these blessings shall come on thee, and overtake thee, if thou shalt hearken unto the voice of the LORD thy God.

Blessed shalt thou be in the city, and blessed shalt thou be in the field.

Blessed shall be the fruit of thy body, and the fruit of thy ground, and the fruit of thy cattle, the increase of thy kine, and the flocks of thy sheep.

Blessed shall be thy basket and thy store.

Blessed shalt thou be when thou comest in,

above all nations

and blessed shalt thou be when thou goest out.

The LORD shall cause thine enemies that rise up against thee to be smitten before thy face: they shall come out against thee one way, and flee before thee seven ways.

The LORD shall command the blessing upon thee in thy storehouses, and in all that thou settest thine hand unto; and he shall bless thee in the land which the LORD thy God giveth thee.

The LORD shall establish thee an holy people unto himself, as he hath sworn unto thee, if thou shalt keep the commandments of the LORD thy God, and walk in his ways."

- Deuteronomy 28: 1-9

an holy people

Abraham Lincoln was asked which side God was on in the Civil War. He responded: "I am not at all concerned about that, for I know that the Lord is always on the side of right. But it is my constant anxiety and prayer that I and this nation should be on the Lord's side." (Abraham Lincoln's Stories and Speeches, J.B. McClure, ed. [Chicago: Rhodes and McClure Publishing Co., 1896], pp. 185-86)

on the Lord's side

"Our constitution was made only for a
moral and religious people. It is wholly
inadequate to the government of any
other." (John Adams, In John R. Howe, Jr.'s,
The Changing Political Thought of John Adams
[Princeton: Princeton University Press,
1966], p. 185)

"God, who gave us life, gave us liberty.
Can the liberties of a nation be secure when
we have removed a conviction that these
liberties are a gift of God?" (Thomas
Jefferson, *In Love with Eloquence*, p. 30)

only for a moral people

America Too Proud?

"We have grown in numbers, wealth and power as no other nation has ever grown. But we have forgotten God. We have forgotten the gracious hand which preserved us in peace and multiplied and enriched and strengthened us; and we have vainly imagined, in the deceitfulness of our hearts, that all these blessings were produced by some superior wisdom and virtue of our own. Intoxicated with unbroken success, we have become too self-sufficient to feel the necessity of redeeming and preserving grace, too proud to pray to the God that made us!"
(Abraham Lincoln, *A Proclamation "to designate and set apart a day for National prayer and humiliation."*)

to proud to pray?

"America, under the smiles of a Divine Providence, the protection of a good government, and the cultivation of manners, morals, and piety, cannot fail of attaining an uncommon degree of eminence, in literature, commerce, agriculture, improvements at home and respectability abroad."

- George Washington

uncommon eminence

With Liberty

Patrick Henry
1736-1799

*"Is life so dear, or peace so sweet, as to be
purchased at the price of chains and slavery? - I
know not what course others may take; but as for
me, give me liberty or give me death."*

- Patrick Henry

liberty or death

Let Freedom Ring

"This nation came into being only through freedom of choice, sacrifice, labor, and struggle. Brave Americans gave their lives in the settlement of this nation -- and in its preservation. Let us remember our heritage and recognize that the day of courage, labor, and sacrifice is never done. For the welfare of America, each citizen must develop a keener sense of responsibility for the solution of public questions -- all public questions.

"Our people must think. They must discuss. They must have the courage of their convictions. They must decide on a course of action and they must follow through. All this must be done freely, in the open, without government dictation or control." (Ezra Taft Benson, _The Red Carpet_ p. 312; see also _Teachings of Ezra Taft Benson_ p. 579)

sense of responsibility

The Great Charter of Liberty

Early "Americans adhered rather closely to the free market ideal that people should remain free to find their own solutions for economic problems, whether caused by industry or by nature. The force of government would be used, if deemed necessary, only at the local level, under local control, to meet local needs. And as a result, America became a new promised land.

"We later Americans have all but forfeited the great charter of liberty that made possible the miracle of America. It still exists for us to examine. If we still like it, we can reestablish it. Doing that will require as much persistence and dedication and plain hard work on our part as was required of the eighteenth-century gentlemen who created it. It will require as much labor to regain it as it did to create it, but thankfully not more."(Lawrence Patton McDonald, *We Hold These Truths, p. 14-15,* '76 Press, 1976)

miracle of America

"The Spirit of the Lord GOD is upon me; because the Lord hath anointed me to preach good tidings unto the meek; he hath sent me to bind up the brokenhearted, to proclaim liberty to the captives, and the opening of the prison to them that are bound;"

- Isaiah 61:1

proclaim liberty

Keeping Our Freedom

"The only way we can keep our freedom is to work at it. Not some of us. All of us. Not some of the time, but all of the time." (Spencer W. Kimball, Teachings of Spencer W. Kimball, chapter 15, p. 405, par 7)

all of us, all of the time

"Congress shall make no law respecting an establishment of religion, or prohibiting the free exercise thereof; or abridging the freedom of speech, or of the press; or the right of the people peaceably to assemble, and to petition the Government for a re-dress of grievances."

- U.S. Constitution
1st Amendment

religion, speech, press

"The liberty of the press is indeed essential to the nature of a free state; but this consists in laying no previous restraints upon publication, and not in freedom from censure from criminal matter when published. Every freeman has an undoubted right to lay what sentiments he pleases before the public: to forbid this, is to destroy the freedom of the press: but if he publishes what is improper, mischievous, or illegal, he must take the consequence of his own temerity. To subject the press to the restrictive power of a licenser... is to subject all freedom of sentiment to the prejudice of [whatever agency has the power to issue or withhold the license]." (Blackstone's Commentaries as quoted by Lawrence Patton McDonald in *We Hold These Truths, p. 42,* '76 Press, 1976)

𝔩𝔦𝔟𝔢𝔯𝔱𝔶 𝔬𝔣 𝔱𝔥𝔢 𝔭𝔯𝔢𝔰𝔰

"The right of the people to be secure in their persons, houses, papers, and effects, against unreasonable searches and seizures, shall not be violated, and no Warrants shall issue, but upon probable cause, supported by Oath or affirmation, and particularly describing the place to be searched, and the persons or things to be seized."

- U.S. Constitution
4th Amendment

search & seizure

"A well regulated Militia, being necessary to the security of a free State, the right of the people to keep and bear Arms, shall not be infringed."

> \- U.S. Constitution
> 2nd Amendment

"No Soldier shall, in time of peace be quartered in any house, without the consent of the Owner, nor in time of war, but in a manner to be prescribed by law."

> \- U.S. Constitution
> 3rd Amendment

right to bear arms

"The enumeration in the Constitution, of certain rights, shall not be construed to deny or disparage others retained by the people."

- U.S. Constitution
  9th Amendment

"The powers not delegated to the United States by the Constitution, nor prohibited by it to the States, are reserved to the States respectively, or to the people."

- U.S. Constitution
  10th Amendment

uncommon eminence

America the Beautiful

America! America!
God mend thine every flaw,
Confirm thy soul in self-control
Thy liberty in law.

   - Katherine Lee Bates

liberty in law

"I thank God that I have lived to see my country independent and free. She may long enjoy her independence and freedom if she will. It depends upon her virtue." (Samuel Adams, Wells, *The Life of Samuel Adams*, 3:175)

𝔡𝔢𝔭𝔢𝔫𝔡𝔰 𝔲𝔭𝔬𝔫 𝔥𝔢𝔯 𝔳𝔦𝔯𝔱𝔲𝔢

Beware of Surrendering Your Liberty

"A people may prefer a free government, but if, from indolence, or carelessness, or cowardice, or want of public spirit, they are unequal to the exertions necessary for preserving it; if they will not fight for it when it is directly attacked; if they can be deluded by the artifices used to cheat them out of it; if by momentary discouragement, or temporary panic, or a fit of enthusiasm for an individual, they can be induced to lay their liberties at the feet even of a great man, or trust him with powers which enable him to subvert their institutions; in all these cases they are more or less unfit for liberty: and though it may be for their good to have had it even for a short time, they are unlikely long to enjoy it." (John Stuart Mill, *Considerations on Representative Government* [London:Parker, Son, and Bourn, West Strand., 1861], p.6)

being fit for liberty

"Where the Spirit of the Lord is, there is liberty."

  - 2 Corinthians 3:17

"And I will walk at liberty: for I seek thy precepts."

  - Psalms 119:45

Spirit brings liberty

"Men are qualified for civil liberty in exact
proportion to their disposition to put moral
chains on their own appetites... Society
cannot exist unless a controlling power
upon the will and appetite be placed some-
where, and the less of it there is within, the
more there must be without. It is ordained
in the eternal constitution of things, that
men of intemperate minds cannot be free.
Their passions forge their fetters."
(Edmund Burke, *The Works of Edmund
Burke*, vol. 4, Waltham, Mass.: Little,
Brown, 1866, pp. 51-52)

who can be free?

Alexander Hamilton 1755-1804

"Safety from external danger is the most powerful director of national conduct. Even the ardent love of liberty will, after a time, give way to its dictates. The violent destruction of life and property incident to war, the continual effort and alarm attendant on a state of continual danger, will compel nations the most attached to liberty to resort for repose and security to institutions which have a tendency to destroy their civil and political rights. To be more safe, they at length become willing to run the risk of being less free." (Alexander Hamilton, as quoted in W. Cleon Skousen's *The Making of America*, p. 237)

danger to liberty

"Liberty exists in proportion to wholesome restraining."

- Daniel Webster

"Government is not reason, it is not eloquence -- it is force! Like fire, it is a dangerous servant and a fearful master!"

- George Washington

a fearful master

"Stand fast therefore in the liberty where-
with Christ hath made us free, and be not
entangled again with the yoke of bond-
age."

 - Galations 5:1

stand fast in the liberty

"The end of law is not to abolish or restrain, but to preserve and enlarge freedom. For in all the states of created beings, capable of laws, where there is no law there is no freedom. For liberty is to be free from restraint and violence from others, which cannot be where there is no law; and is not, as we are told, 'a liberty for every man to do what he lists.' For who could be free, when every other man's humor might domineer over him? But a liberty to dispose and order freely as he lists his person, actions, possessions, and his whole property within the allowance of those laws under which he is, and therein not to be subject to the arbitrary will of another, but freely follow his own." (John Locke, *Two Treatises, Book 2, no. 57*)

enlarge freedom

And Justice for All

"He hath shewed thee, O man, what is good; and what doth the Lord require of thee, but to do justly, and to love mercy, and to walk humbly with thy God?"

    - *Micah 6: 8*

to do justly

"No person shall be held to answer for a capital, or otherwise infamous crime, unless on a presentment or indictment of a Grand Jury, except in cases arising in the land or naval forces, or in the Militia, when in actual service in time of War or public danger; nor shall any person be subject for the same offence to be twice put in jeopardy of life or limb; nor shall be compelled in any criminal case to be a witness against himself, nor be deprived of life, liberty, or property, without due process of law; nor shall private property be taken for public use, without just compensation."

          - U.S. Constitution
          5th Amendment

due process of law

"In all criminal prosecutions, the accused shall enjoy the right to a speedy and public trial, by an impartial jury of the State and district wherein the crime shall have been committed, which district shall have been previously ascertained by law, and to be informed of the nature and cause of the accusation; to be confronted with the witnesses against him; to have compulsory process for obtaining witnesses in his favor, and to have the Assistance of Counsel for his defence."

> \- U.S. Constitution
> 6th Amendment

speedy and public trial

"In Suits at common law, where the value in controversy shall exceed twenty dollars, the right of trial by jury shall be preserved, and no fact tried by a jury, shall be otherwise reexamined in any Court of the United States, than according to the rules of the common law."

- U.S. Constitution
7th Amendment

"Excessive bail shall not be required, nor excessive fines imposed, nor cruel and unusual punishments inflicted."

- U.S. Constitution
8th Amendment

trial by jury

"Justice and judgment are the habitation of thy throne: mercy and truth shall go before thy face."

   - Psalms 89:14

"Thus saith the LORD, Keep ye judgment, and do justice: for my salvation is near to come, and my righteousness to be revealed."

   - Isaiah 56: 1

justice and judgement

"In the Declaration of Independence Thomas Jefferson had written that 'all men...are endowed by their Creator with certain unalienable rights...[and] to secure these rights, governments are instituted.'

"When a government protects the rights of its people and provides an adequate remedy for those whose rights have been violated, then that government is providing equal justice for all.

"Justice requires an opportunity and a place to complain of an injury as well as the machinery to provide a remedy. For the accused, justice requires the opportunity to hear and understand the charge, cross-examine those who are making the charge, have a fair and speedy trial, and have an opportunity to repair the wrong if found guilty.

"Nothing destroys the credibility of a government faster than its failure to provide fair and equal justice for its people." (W. Cleon Skousen, *The Making of America*, p 239, National Center for Constitutional Studies, 1986)

fair & equal justice

"Yet they seek me daily, and delight to know my ways, as a nation that did righteousness, and forsook not the ordinance of their God: they ask of me the ordinances of justice; they take delight in approaching to God."

   - Isaiah 58: 2

ordinances of justice

"I believe... that [justice] is instinctive and innate, that the moral sense is as much a part of our constitution as that of feeling, seeing, or hearing; as a wise Creator must have seen to be necessary in an animal destined to live in society; that every human mind feels pleasure in doing good to another; that the nonexistence of justice is not to be inferred from the fact that the same act is deemed virtuous and right in one society which is held vicious and wrong in another; because, as the circumstances and opinions of different societies vary, so the acts which may do them right or wrong must vary also; for virtue does not consist in the act we do, but in the end it is to effect. If it is to effect the happiness of him to whom it is directed, it is virtuous, while in a society under different circumstances and opinions, the same act might produce pain, and would be vicious. The essence of virtue is in doing good to others, while what is good may be one thing in one society, and its contrary in another." (Thomas Jefferson quoted in W. Cleon Skousen's *The Making of America*, p. 240)

justice - an inborn sense

Thomas Jefferson

"I deem [one of] the essential principles of our government, and consequently [one] which ought to shape its administration,... equal and exact justice to all men, of whatever state or persuasion, religious or political." (Thomas Jefferson as quoted in W. Cleon Skousen's *The Making of America*, p 241)

equal and exact justice

"When one under-
takes to administer
justice, it must be
with an even hand,
and by rule; what is
done for one must be
done for everyone in
equal degree."
(Thomas Jefferson as
quoted in W. Cleon
Skousen's *The Mak-
ing of America*, p 241)

an even hand

"I have often pondered over the dangers
which were incurred by the men who
assembled here and framed and adopted
that Declaration. I have pondered over the
toils that were endured by the officers and
soldiers of the army who achieved that
independence. I have often inquired of
myself what great principle or idea it was
that kept this Confederacy so long together.
It was not the mere matter of separation of
the colonies from the motherland, but that
sentiment in the Declaration of Independence which gave liberty not alone to the
people of this country, but hope to all the
world, for all future time. It was that which
gave promise that in due time the weights
would be lifted from the shoulders of all
men, and that all should have an equal
chance. This is the sentiment embodied in
the Declaration of Independence."
(Abraham Lincoln, Independence Hall,
February 22, 1861)

hope to all the world

"What constitutes the bulwark of our own liberty and independence? It is not our frowning battlements, our bristling seacoasts... our reliance is in the love of liberty which God has planted in us. Our defense is in the spirit which prized liberty as the heritage of all men, in all lands every-where." (Abraham Lincoln, *In Love With Eloquence*, p. 33)

heritage of all men

"The cause of America is in great measure
the cause of all mankind"

- Thomas Paine, *Common Sense*

𝔠𝔞𝔲𝔰𝔢 𝔬𝔣 𝔞𝔩𝔩 𝔪𝔞𝔫𝔨𝔦𝔫𝔡

A Concluding Prayer for America

"O God, our Eternal Father, Thou who presides over the nations and their people, we come unto Thee in prayer. We thank Thee for this great and sovereign nation of which we are citizens. Touch the minds of those of our Congress that they shall stand tall and independent in defense of the liberty of the people. Bless the Chief Executive. He is our president. Let Thy Spirit move upon him to bring to pass those measures which will lift the burdens of government from the backs of the people and keep this nation, under God, a citadel of freedom standing as an example to all the world. Bless the Supreme Court of the United States, which in recent days has declared unconstitutional a measure designed to secure the religious liberty of the people of this nation. May a way be found under Thy divine inspiration to bring to pass another measure which will be sustained by the Court.

May Thy peace rest upon this nation. May we as a people look to Thee and live. May the benevolent hand of the Almighty protect us from the evil forces of the world. May humanism and secularism bend to an increased acknowledgment of Thee as our Father and our God.

May a spirit of brotherhood spread throughout the land.

As we pray to Thee we do so in our manner, and respect the prayers of others who speak after their manner, that Thou will hear us all as we lift our voices in behalf of our nation. Almighty Father, hear us, guide us, protect us. Make us both strong and benevolent before the world. Forgive our erring ways. May we turn back to Thee in our search for wisdom, for guidance, for direction, we humbly ask in the name of Jesus Christ, amen."

- Gordon B. Hinckley
"Our Nations True Source of Strength"
Address given 29 June 1997

Author Index

www.ingramcontent.com/pod-product-compliance
Lightning Source LLC
Chambersburg PA
CBHW022120280326
41933CB00007B/469